THE *Softness* OF THE WORD

Reflections of a Ten Year Old

SARA EDGAR

ISBN: 1-4392-3673-9

ISBN-13: 9781439236734

Visit www.booksurge.com to order additional copies.

Acknowledgements

To Jeannie Follet who asked me to proof read her children's book. It planted the seed that I could create a book too. Thanks Jeannie!

To Dorsey Baumgartner who put the first draft together for me. I really could see it happening, the book. Thanks Dorsey!

To my cousin Kelly for using her great computer knowledge to get the book to the publisher. Thanks Kelly!

To all my family and friends who said, "You can do it, Sara!" and even to all those who said it would never happen… I saw it and did it anyway!

INTRODUCTION

As a parent you know of the softness of the Word. At times you hear it when you are calm…when you are at peace. Often you are not certain why… you just feel it. Usually it comes to you when you are very quiet. Shh…

Can you hear it? It is in this moment that we take a deep breath and fill ourselves with beautiful thoughts. Our intention becomes of love and we begin to learn a new way of life.

Some will say

She is just ten…what does she know?

Some will say

I already know these things…

And Sara will say to you…

Until you live something each day and it becomes a part of you…

Do you really know it?

THE COFFEE SHOP

THE COFFEE SHOP

One day in a coffee shop I saw a little girl looking at a beautiful bracelet for sale. I watched as she walked toward it smiling. Before she could reach for it, her Mom yelled… "DON'T TOUCH IT!! You know better than that!" What if her Mom had just said … "Let me help you see that beautiful bracelet?" It was so beautiful…she just wanted to touch it. After her Mom yelled at her, she stood behind a chair as if she wanted to hide. Her Mom kept talking about how they had to hurry.

Sometimes I think hurrying keeps Moms and Dads from the softness of the Word.

When there is something beautiful it is ok to take time to enjoy it. Always ask first!

GOING FOR A WALK

Sara Edgar

GOING FOR A WALK

Sometimes I like going for a walk. I smell the fresh air....I listen to the birds.....It just makes me feel good. What if people just took walks with one another...not saying anything...Just taking a walk...

Could that help them to be softer with their words?

Walking quietly with a friend can be fun!

MY FRIEND FELL DOWN

MY FRIEND FELL DOWN

Whoops! It was a good one….she tripped and feel right in the middle of the play ground. Everyone said for her to get up, for her just to be tough. Well I understand being tough. She got up but I think her feelings and her knee hurt a lot. Something inside of me just knew that she wanted someone to say "You all right?" I helped her up and she smiled and said thanks. Then she was smiling again.

I guess the Softness of the Word sometimes can be just three words…you all right?

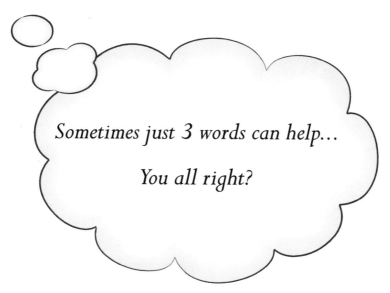

Sometimes just 3 words can help…

You all right?

ALL ABOUT HAIR OR IS IT?

ALL ABOUT HAIR OR IS IT?

I wonder sometimes where words come from. Why we do not see how words can be hurtful or soft. When I watch others I can learn.

One day a boy said to my friend, "Boy your hair is red! Really Weird!" She cried. Where did those words come from? Is he just mean? Did he want our attention? I don't understand why people treat each other the way that they do sometimes.

Maybe it does not matter why… Maybe the words that people say belong to them…They only hurt us if we allow them to. Cool HUH?

I will be very careful with the things I say …I guess that is the Softness of the Word too. I will practice taking a little breath before I say something to someone today.

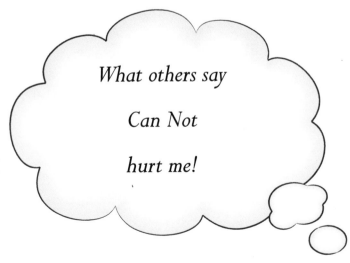

What others say

Can Not

hurt me!

THE NEW BIKE

THE NEW BIKE

My friend was so happy! She had a bright and shiny new bike! She had dreamed of it for months! She cut out pictures of bikes. No matter where we went she would say, "That's just like the bike I will be getting soon!" She finally got it!

We rode over to the playground so that everyone could see it! Most of the kids said, "So what…we have had our bikes for two years." That's nothing.

This little voice inside of me said to tell her that it was the most beautiful bike I had ever seen! It was like magic! She rode off smiling and tomorrow we are going to ride bikes together! Sometimes I get a little tired because people do not see how easy that it is to help each other be happy….

I think today I will use just a few words… and for those who do not understand the Softness of the Word… well, I can just walk away from them. Whew, sometimes they do make me tired!

Remember it is good to be glad for others!

THE CYNIC

THE CYNIC

A person who's beliefs all are motivated by selfishness.

I had to look that one up. Sometimes I wonder if it would be better to use just a few words. Or maybe just to send the feeling of love to someone. We can do that you know. I asked my Mom how come grownups say a lot, "Yeah right that will never happen. Ha!" She said that they were cynics. I looked it up. It didn't feel very good to think that is how a lot of people see the world. I think I would rather be a person who sees that anything is possible! Once I had a friend call me a "Goody Two Shoes". I think she meant because I always see most things as really neat. I kind of love all people. I'm really not sure what she meant but I think I would rather be known as Sara Happy Feet! Get it?

See the Softness of the Word?

Anything

is

Possible!!

HAPPY OR SAD?

HAPPY OR SAD

My teacher taught me this. I can be happy or sad. I used to think if my friend Kevin was mean to me or my friends at school were in a bad mood that was about me too. I have heard grownups say, "I can tell what kind of a day this is going to be!" I almost believed them! My teacher says that we can be happy or sad. She says it is that simple. If I stubbed my toe and say, "I can see it now. The rest of my day is ruined, it will be just that! Or I can put a band-aid on my toe and start again. I can turn my day around. I will think of something beautiful, a cute puppy.

It is like using the Softness of the Word just for me. And today will be the most beautiful day! I think it feels much better to be happy! So I can choose to be happy or sad. I like that!

I can **CHOOSE** *to be* **HAPPY**

So there it is…

And I will say to you…

Have a beautiful day!

You are perfect as you are!

And yes I am ten years old and

I do know of The Softness of the Word

Because I am living it!

With Much Love,

Sara

ABOUT THE AUTHOR

Sara Edgar is now 11 years old and lives in Bucks County, Pennsylvania. She is a dancer, cyclist and loves all sports. Sara attends United Friends School in Quakertown Pennsylvania where she enjoys their thoughts of peace and working on ideas to save the planet. Sara invites you to contact her at sasedgar@cs.com if you are an aspiring young author with questions or if you just need someone to say "You can do it!"

OK...now it's your turn.

Use the following pages

to write down some ideas

about how YOU can choose

to live the Softness of the Word.

Remember it only works

if you really live it.

Made in the USA
Charleston, SC
27 February 2010